T0266080

A YEAR IN THE NEW LIFE

by the same author

poetry
HAPPINESS

JACK UNDERWOOD

A Year in the New Life

faber

First published in 2021
by Faber & Faber Ltd
Bloomsbury House
74–77 Great Russell Street
London WC1B 3DA

First published in the USA in 2021

Typeset by Hamish Ironside
Printed in the UK by TJ Books Ltd, Padstow, Cornwall

All rights reserved
© Jack Underwood, 2021

The right of Jack Underwood to be identified as author of this work
has been asserted in accordance with Section 77 of the Copyright,
Designs and Patents Act 1988

A CIP record for this book is available from the British Library

ISBN 978–0–571–36725–2

FSC
www.fsc.org
MIX
Paper from
responsible sources
FSC® C013056

10 9 8 7 6 5 4 3

For Nancy Agnes

Acknowledgements

I would like to thank the editors of the following magazines and journals for publishing some of these poems: *Poetry Review*, *Granta*, *Poetry London*, *White Review*, *The Rialto*, *POETRY*, *The Believer*, *Apology*, *Jubilat & Wildness*. I am grateful to my friends and family in poems for their kindness, support and excellent heads, especially Emily Berry, Robert Herbert McClean, Holly Pester, Ben Pester, Sam Riviere, Rachael Allen, Heather Phillipson, Joe Dunthorne, Wayne Holloway-Smith, Katherine Kilalea, Luke Kennard, Anthony Anaxagorou, Sophie Collins, Rachel Long, Raymond Antrobus, Maura Dooley, Maurice Riordan, Inua Ellams, Elaine Kahn, Jiaoyang Li, Morgan Parker, Kaveh Akbar, Paige Lewis, Matthew Rohrer, Ocean Vuong, Zain Aslam and Emily Toder. I would also like to thank everyone at Faber for being so patient and good, in particular Matthew Hollis, Lavinia Singer and Hannah Marshall, and as ever I am indebted to my agent, Harriet Moore, for lifting great weights and sorting things out. I would like to thank my family for their love and buoying, and most of all, Hannah and Nancy, for being best, and sharing The New Life with me.

Contents

A YEAR IN THE NEW LIFE

Errata

My grandfather, dying, explained
that *letting go* is the easy part;
you can only do half the job,
the rest, he said, is up to God,
or time, which is the same thing,
though I'm sure I've not remembered
or measured it correctly, maybe
someone else's grandfather or
crossing a border on horseback or
was it, then, a butterfly already on
the wing, the fog was rising – *I must
go in* – but in this version a boat
is getting quietly away at night,
a rope hauled through dark water
by a hand that reaches to find
the edge of a table, and retreats,
nothing permanent upturned.

Poem Beginning with Lines by Elizabeth Barrett Browning

But I could not hide
My quickening inner life from those at watch.
They saw a light at a window now and then,
They had not set there. Who had set it there?
Not me. I'm just a slug on the wet inner face
of the discourse, chirpsing the wind;
I've no idea what drags the chair, bruises
the fruit, leads a child towards a dead rabbit
and bids them not weep, nor laugh, but sing.
My childhood neighbour recalled how I rode
my bike down the hill beside our house,
and practised my dying; arranging my body
in the bushes, lying still. All summer I did it,
repeating the drama, which is how a song
is made; you make a phrase and turn it
over and over like a dead rabbit, finding on
the other side, o look, this rabbit, dead, too.

A girl or woman in relation to either or both
of her parents

also *noun* meaning weather as in I expect the good
daughter won't last or the daughter is likely to improve
at the weekend also *verb* meaning to become aware
of one's overwhelmedness as in we were daughtered
by the magnitude of the cave system also *adj* meaning
robust as in such behaviour was met with a daughter
response also *noun* meaning overseer as in a daughter
was assigned by the company to assess whose work
had been completed satisfactorily also *noun* meaning
metal jug for outdoor use as in we arrived at the shed
and the daughter was already full of autumn leaves
also *noun* meaning a situation that forces the mind
to conceive of the impossible as in suddenly we had
a daughter and it began to rain indoors.

An Envelope

What about days when you feel nothing.
Waiting in the car, relative arbitration,
pigeon-pewter or urinal-cake sky, whatever.
A man shouting, a parade of missiles . . .

You chew the food and harvest thoughts
from a sea floor. Control subject,
a raincoat blurred in closed-circuit resolution,
you pinch the nerveless flesh

of your elbows and fail to love well.
You try to carry a flag, at least,
in the distance. This is not sickness.
This is not anything. Hand gripping

the big knife cutting onions. You could
cut fifty onions this way. You could sleep
until Easter. Maybe the fog will have lifted
by then and time will not seem to pass

like small bones being broken in order.
What's that sound? Bald human instinct,
pounding on the windows like a fly.
Who am I? All blown open, paper fold,

you cannot stop the living obligations,
debts abstracting in neutral waves.
Please come back. Patient hearts
are lining up along the shore.

A Year in the New Life

It was winter. The counterpart of burning,
which is also burning.
My banner displayed clock parts,
a cup of wine, a worm eating its opposite head.
My motto was *try to be responsible*,
but every new moon was a sacrificial moon.
Thirteen paving slabs were flipped into the river.

The extra light of spring threw our business
into relief. My banner displayed a sunburst,
a bloodied hand dropping a knife, and
in the other hand an avocado withholding
its stone. War would soon come but not
for us, and this became our motto, *not for us*.
Then a crime in our community led to anger.
Gossip gathered the truth into a ball,
paperwork was spoiled, a man was removed
from the yellow light of the barn.
We heard his sobs coming from the orchard,
and these were a source of comfort.

Summer roused lanterns of dust under doorways,
though a vinegar taste kept the air difficult.
Antifa angels bathed their eyes in milk,
as horses refused riders. The timid among us
signed petitions swearing that when the time came
we would know it by the rocks in our hands.
I made a banner for the protests to come
depicting the planting of milk teeth,
the unfolding of a noose, a stadium left empty.

Autumn was just my luck. I could not stomach
the broth I boiled, and slept badly.
Arguments I won in my head lost direction
when formed out loud. The riots continued
but quietly now, indoors.
It was a time for manifestos, though the wrongs
were too many for anything less than a lake.
Friends kept the counsel of friends.
In the yellow light of the barn we tried to write
sentences each other would like, or not desire
to alter. Together we designed a quilt depicting
the wolf taking scent, water moving quickly,
the sign of the errant cloud and alphabet,
a baby resisting sleep, a worm eating
its opposite head, only this time surrounded
by snow, which hasn't stopped falling since
Thursday, the name we gave to our child.

Poem Beginning with a Line by Anna Seward

But oh with pale, and warring fires, decline
the waking tasks, if that's what you need.
You don't have to compete with business.
You don't have to compete with me, moving things
from room to room, nurturing distraction.
Shut the hillside behind you. Burn whichever forest.
I can water the smouldering animals.
If you need me to tie your hair back, I will learn
to tie your hair back well. If you need me to pass
this week over to the saints, I will guide them
through orientation. If you are unsure
what you want from life, and include me
in that confusion, I can still offer water,
or else go back downstairs to sit and stir,
on your behalf, this brilliant white emulsion.

The Landing

for Nancy Agnes

You come / round thinking
in a new language / of the familiar
your voice / dragging at my body
my body / still waking
but already / I'm on the landing
I'm reaching you / awake now
my hand / in the black
finding the back / of your sweaty
little head / *I'm here I'm here* . . .
to settle / you again
into sleep / and inside
your neat organs / are working
your lungs / I can hear
are filling / with the air
the food / in your stomach
I cooked you / today
the piss / in your bladder
and the shit / in your colon
your pancreas / your liver
like the offal / of a songbird
dark and busy / and your feet
like rare cave mushrooms
your eyelashes / and hair
which you've grown / from nothing
made / for yourself
for your life / by your mother
from nothing / and I'm filled
I'm filled / with the fear
of the joy / no the sadness

of the joy / a leaf
on a street / what I mean
if you don't know / what I mean
by the sadness / of the joy
is forgive me / I mean don't worry
about it / for a second
if you don't / but if you do
know what I mean / and I'm still
alive to tell / please
please come / and tell me
about it / I'm here
I'm here / I'll never leave this room.

War the War

War the war, the sorry edge
of us, because we stacked nice

clean plates for days we were
sure things when love broke

across the headland, leaving
conch shells in ditches,

five fish slapping on the steps
of the old town hall, it was winter,

we were bonfires unattended,
our bodies litigating, agreeing

and writing it all down, the law
of legs, the law of how we sleep,

the law of shoulders killing me
and now we fold clothes without

thinking *my clothes your clothes*
and war the war o happy war

what love we are so badly bitten
in this long-term necessary chapel

with all attendant relics, citronella
candle, junior hacksaw,

a box of miscellaneous wires,
our headland way way underwater,

no one else beside us
but ourselves beside ourselves.

Please and Thank You

There isn't one of us standing on this platform
who hasn't looked down and
thought about it. Even a child's mind wanders
that way, as nature wanders
into a golf course, as words drift across
a prairie, as names settle down and roost,
and there is always a night-time
about to happen somewhere,
someone wading into a shallow sleep
in pursuit of symbolic problems,
as a mourner wades into the present,
as a husband wades into the sea looking
for a mobile phone. What if one of us turned
to say, *Compared to you other people are just*
dry brushes in a jar. Would it make
a difference? Can't we all just come
to a wider arrangement, heaving
our blood to the rhythm of a cat
washing thoroughly, like
thank you thank you thank you,
declaring how dignified it felt to stand
in place this morning *thank you thank you*
and dignified to keep our thoughts
so quiet and close together?

I am become a man

with fats around my organs lightly
hair grown on my shoulders
lightly death in all my actions as I build
a log-store shirtless in the autumn.

I hate this gathering and deepening
beneath my pale tabard; boyhood gone
and with it all my girlishness: hands-
on-the-headphones-dance-move/
lasso-move-and-shimmy; now my hips
thrust solemn as lorries gather in a layby
to discuss my remaining options.

I cannot leave the barbecue unsupervised
as I focus on ignoring my body
in the changing rooms. Not one
of the maximum eight permitted items
fits me nicely. Handsome is for horses,
house plants, hotels, tall and deco
in dreamy pastel shades.

I've never wanted to fight anyone
ever, or be real this way and mean it.
I just want to bellow love unbridled,
an elk beneath an overpass, and retire
my life gently, so that capable hands
need not lift much soil or sadness.

Fifteen Babies in My Garden

each at a different stage in their development,
including a fully grown adult baby, all of them
sitting around, or lying, or trying to turn
over onto their fronts, or back onto their backs,
the sunshine apple-scented, the still trees
monastic, as I carry a large tray of drinks
out to them: different milks in different
bottles I've sterilised, and, for the adult baby,
an Old Fashioned in a tumbler, orange peel
suspended in amber, a black cherry blot.
'Here you go, babies!' I say, and they coo
and squirm and gripe and sleep regress.
'What are you guys talking about?' I ask,
and the adult baby, being the best speaker
among them and therefore, I suppose,
their designated spokesperson, replies,
'We were just talking about the ruinous
and beautiful ways we're going to break
your dumb old heart, and totally fuck
your life up' and they all start laughing.

This Has No Sound

I was on the boulevard of burning sycamores
cars sinking like swamp creatures tyres
giving out in a sequence of gasps
streetlamps drooping like tulips a dot
of mercury on my forehead I was ready
to admit my symptoms
and recognise love as precision gratitude
and feeling woozy from the fumes I suffered
a sudden loss of weight I mean I suffered
a sudden weightlessness the ash falling and
rising as I stood on the white-hot kerb
and sucked my thumb
it was two hours or days before
I woke surrounded by an adolescent rain
that touched my surfaces darker
and I knew then I could walk from this world
like a customer
I could walk from this world like a customer
a fox and hounds to be
continued to be or not a fox and
many hounds.

My name is zonal coordinator

Listen to my voice happening inside you.
Feel the way I pronounce these words,
moving them through you like fruits
of different sizes and shapes. *Apricot.*
I'm going to move the word *apricot*
to touch against your liver. Is that OK?
Do you know where your liver is?
Apricot. There, you've found it.
You are beginning to feel lighter.
You are on a generic tropical beach.
Your wisdom teeth are calm and happy.
Your family forgives you. You are lava
rising through the mantle of the world
oblivious to events upon its surface.
Your friends like you. You are floating.
My peregrine will guide you.
See small adjustments to her wing-tips.
Nothing is holding you up now.
The second digit of your security number
has fallen far away. No one is cross
with you. The world will return
to its natural state of non-existence,
but only when you do. Repeat after me:
I am feeling so good about myself.
I am feeling so good about myself.

Prolactin

Now I am even softer.
Not just the Christmas commercials,
I cry to reggae.
I cry on my way to the shop
so I have to go to the further shop
to give myself more time.

I am nearly beautiful, pressed against an edge
I cannot name.
I am beautiful about all the things
I can do with my hands for other people.

How much love do I have inside me now?
As in the effect of mass on the curvature
of space-time, or? OK, OK, something
you can see. Maybe

rapeseed yellow,
every day,
the whole fucking field.

The Long Twenty-first Century

I took your letter into the field
to read again in my heaviest gown.
It was drizzly as I waded in lavender
thigh-high and moved my lips
hoping to make the shapes
your lips had made, and, lying
down to star-jump my legs
apart, I pictured you sweating
several hundred years like this,
dry-licking your teeth, horny
with emotion, keeping your
centre of gravity low and low
to brace against the boom-song
of my faint ordnance. *Sorry,
what song?* This song: incoming.

My body is a good body

a wild instrument and family meal,
tender and attentive slap-up mammal,
steadying a shelf, and, with my free hand
in your hand, my body is meanwhile meat,
stress-eating granola or carrying your unique
weight across the afternoon, all systems
failing in threat computation; stumbling
hungry from the churn, a froth moustache
and prehistoric horn erect; top orca;
bullock of the moon; punished god, quiet
and blurry on the sofa, the cartoon's happy
ending got my throat all thick. Listen, darlings,
Death is always better prepared than we are,
a boy scout of coincidence and indeterminate
religion. So I'm not going to sit around here
all day not being sentimental. I am nothing
but yours to take and take, this unholy loaf,
this boat, a boy stood on its burning deck,
suddenly grown up, waving at you.

Poem Beginning with Lines by Ye Hongxiang

Adapted from the translation by Kang-I Sun Chang and Charles Kwong

I've leaned towards the edge of the sky along the curved
    railings;
where the sun falls aslant on the gaunt green hills . . .
How will I survive the moonrise for one more evening,
or the sound of dew dripping from my leaking parasol
when it would be so much easier to die and die
and keep on dying? To factor the losses: sorely missed,
or not so much; returning more determined to love,
or not so much; nothing but a light, baroque sleep,
empty for the fire, for the mulch . . . A year, a month,
a cool day later, then back upon the threshold,
breathing deep, and welcome, full of contrition, air
and water. To think, tomorrow could be another life.

Whatever I have done that was good, I have done
at the bidding of my voices

Twice in the night I woke and warned
the ghosts, *Your surveillance had better be kind.*
But they know my uglies,
my egg whites, how I glow in autumn,
comparatively, as the world dies about me;
how I tend to my five ongoing feuds
like candles in a church;
how I enter each room in my mind
like a soprano.

But once they reach past all this
shame is not the word, this
cold spaghetti; they'll find me at the table,
forks downturned, boiling a rock inside
to keep me safe like anyone,
so I have to admit I'm grateful
for the ghosts' surveillance. I want to be
good, always risking connection, love
and fauna, and believe in keeping still,
and grace, fresh water.
Twice in the night I woke
and thanked them.

What Happened Here?

A great burning happened here.

And what was burned?

People were burned here: some men and women,
though mostly men.

Why were they burned?

They had cartoon thoughts; they drew too narrowly;
they hollowed out a lung in the centre of the town
using hoses that turned slippery from the blood.

Does that justify the burning?

They stuffed their ears with sympathetic meat; they
drowned a baby for its bath water; they stained the
foxes purple and made new words forbidding their
usage pleasurably.

Does that justify the burning?

They stamped on hands; they boarded up their faces;
sung love songs to their errand boys, errand dogs; their
shapes were simple, the shapes of their mouth-holes;
they repainted all the maps and squashed berries into
them, jabbing their fingers blind, thumping range into
a mean, thumping the dough into an opening.

But does this justify the burning?

Yes. In the end the burning was justified.

                              The way you talk scares me.

I mean you no harm.

                                          . . .

I mean you no harm.

                              Were there many burned here?

No. Only a committee or so; only one season; the rest
withered on the edge when we held it to the light.

                              I am very cold. I don't like the air.

Take my coat. The air was never clear.

                              Thank you. My hands are freezing.

Put your hands between mine.

                              You seem tired. Your eyes look baggy.

I am very tired.

                              But your hands are warm.

I warmed them for a long time, as I stood beside the fire.

Blood Clot in a Winter Landscape

I have become closer to the rock,
much to the jealousy of the shadow
of the rock and the sunlight that falls
upon the rock, though none compete
with the damp earth beneath the rock,
the mutual weight of that affection.
But what of the coin put there, on top,
meaning to mean, but what? That a mind
has actioned here? That a motionless love
might be expressed through deliberate
non-verbal gestures? Can we make love,
not in the midst of a winter landscape,
but with the winter landscape itself?
Can I fall afterwards exhausted upon it,
the snow falling exhausted upon me?
Or else be wakened by a clot of blood
in the middle of that winter landscape,
a clot that ushers me to my feet saying,
Come on – there are portals – opening
in your mouth – right now – every word –
another dimension – these are graveside
aggregates – transport and insituate –
I promise you're not dreaming – of elsewhere
– in your body – that both of us should be –

Where to start, how to stop?

Bravo me. In the hallway.
Not real and slow-clapping.

With oven gloves on.
Keep my body indoors.

Let me loaf long silences.
Make my bed. A tower.

Acid rising in the night.
Finger-sweat on the door.

Handles. A speaking hinge.
Dishonest situations.

This one. Distractions.
I want a life laid out.

The skeleton of a whale.
To go to sleep properly.

The bones and everyone.
Standing around.

How much it gave them.
How deep it went.

The Situation

I need to get out of this situation, I said;
to be more like the day-fox
practically blowing smoke rings
out there on the pavement;
to be a numb little virus, or spore
on the wind with my hair tacky,
my swollen hand resting on the edge
of a smear on a napkin; to hardly touch
things, or access an inbox or die on
contact with a purchase order or
fellow demon of the backwash. Hell.
I don't know what Jesus had in mind
when he said, *Let the day's own trouble
be sufficient for the day* all those years ago
with the tigers flashing their flanks
between the arches of the Colosseum
and the older gods in valid circulation,
but I suspect that when he dreamed
of his imperative getting traction on
the future, it wasn't this one that he saw.
Look around. Safety curtains. Death.
The big fourth wall. That's not how
the future, or trouble, work at all.

August Bank Holiday

Reclamation yard suffen or nuffen
chewing down to the last of the barrel
of the twelve-bore thinking about getting
it over with. Another edgeland rum'un fuck,
stringing up a kill beside the kissing gate
and wanking in the combine cab, mid-
field. No one's awake. No one's up for miles.
You change so everything changes but it
doesn't. You change so everything changes
but it doesn't. Hen shed, drum and bass,
USAF overhead. You can still bowl for half
a pig on fete day. You can still ruin your life
doing graveyard buckets GCSE year or
hot-boxing a Corsa up near Harvey's farm.
I don't fucken know. Marv's severed head
still wedged in his motorcycle helmet.
Like a Lego man. How we laughed.
Ha ha ha. One thing I can tell you
about the bleak, the flat, the squally cirrus
like a mind dragged above your head,
is that silence doesn't need to try
too hard out here. Rest of the world?
That way. This way? A brown sun
murking out the bottom of the mere.

White Cliffs

I've haunted history, big white sheet over the heads
of all my ancestors, bucket of piss-warm milk over-
flowing with my average, born always already
in the lobby with my headwind right behind,
a thousand pale uncles lined up on the staircase
offering their hands, the higher the ceiling
the wider my parachute. There is a poison I ingest
that I can't touch or speak to, every word turning
true and apolitical, my name on all the silverware,
my suit of armour rusting, universal waves a-lap-
lap-lapping, universal moon signing off each peak,
as the big lads assemble singing, *O my shitty country
could be any shitty country cross the sea sea sea.*

The Novel

So there's a man, or a woman – OK, a person,
and this person has a problem. Not so much
a problem as a yearning. They live in a city
but yearn for the quiet of the countryside.
No, they yearn for the geometry, the voltage,
the violent anonymity of the city. Or they yearn
for the selfish, fat simplicity of their childhood.
OK, something more specific. They yearn for
the silence that followed the call of the mother-owl
across the misted glade that morning in June.
Or the silence of a blown filament, like a ruined
suspension bridge in a snow globe without snow.
That is the silence the person yearns for.
Only they don't know they yearn for this silence.
Instead they cast around, throwing their yearning
over everything like holy water, not knowing
the attainment of surrogate objects of desire
only frustrates or aggravates their yearning,
since the act of attainment itself eliminates
an object from the category of desire, throwing it
into relief, so that it takes on a figurine aspect,
a repulsive resemblance of the silent moment
that the person does not know they yearn for.
Thus abandoned, the search continues,
the world always ready with fresh and bright
distractions. And this person is just like us.
It could be us. Only it isn't. But you do know
this person. I can tell you that much.
Though of course, I needn't tell you.
You know exactly who I am talking about.

Lambs

Look at us pointing fingers into tree knots
and animal nesting spaces; a too-hard slap
on the back and not wiping properly;
what we do with our bodies in the mirror
is our business, inverted (back bacon etc.)
keeping a breath to ourselves – no shame
in that – but let's not pretend our dicks
don't spend most of the hours the universe
sends soft and curled like the ears of lambs.
O French boy, never slide your arm from
the shoulder of your friend; you bigger
boys, come bury this pet with me.
It's been dead a long, long time.

Instead of Bad News about a Person I Love

I got a letter through the post decreeing my sainthood.
Beatified, I sat down, because this was big news for me.
Bless the television, bless this chair of four wooden legs.
I felt like calling my parents, but thought, in a saintly way,
to do so would be immodest, so instead I opened the curtains.
Rain was washing everything that seemed in need of washing.
A bird landed on a bush and shook water from its wings
and I closed my eyes briefly, acknowledging its small,
hardworking soul, like a microchip destined for heaven.
The cat came in, little devil, and I forgave her, touching
under her chin, sweet child. We watched the news together
and reflected that this was how the world churns
its butter of beginnings and endings in front of the sun.
What good, I wondered laterally, might befall an ancient
tree today? Perhaps merely nothing much. Perhaps a tree
will carry on just as it was. What minerals will develop
unseen in the earth, deep beneath a human tragedy?
Some minerals. Some salty, bright minerals in the dark.
I spent that morning cutting white paper into triangles.
I spent that afternoon staring at my bits, enamoured.
I spent that evening clapping loudly in the garden,
and come bedtime I was ready to write my long email
to the president of the United States of America.

I'm on the boating lake with Sean

I'm gently rowing, and the birds look sewn
to the surface of the water as it undulates to the sound
of Sean talking beautifully about something
I don't really understand. But all I'm picturing
are brown paper bags with little grease spots near
the bottom seams that have recorded the way
sausage rolls have touched them, or the thin waists
of dogs as depicted in medieval hunting frescos, or
a cherub's fat little hand gesturing
to a vista where smiling families are meeting
to picnic with the animals that God
has also saved, or I'm thinking about
the mechanics of bagpipes, the legs and arms
and the round belly and the long neck with its holes.
This has been the best day ever. Sean smiles.
He's wearing shorts, and so am I.
It's sunny! Mine are so short
they may as well be underpants, and I still
don't understand a word that he is saying.

Empathy Class

To demonstrate, the instructor told the group
to *try and kiss each other all at the same time*.
We tried, but there was no way of telling
if we were making simultaneous contact.
No matter how lovely it felt – our faces
gently knocking – we couldn't be sure
we were all kissing each other. *OK. So
you see my point?* We had to admit we did.

Poem Beginning with Lines by Walter Savage Landor

I warm'd both hands before the fire of Life;
It sinks; and I am ready to depart.
I don't know how the aperture works.
If there's a foyer or waiting room, or if
you go straight off. It doesn't trouble me
that I didn't fuck around or win
a haunted heirloom from the panel;
didn't curate my time to reach beyond
the remit of apologetic monologues;
didn't kill any fash like Grandpa, nor
suck my soup through a straw following
a goodly crash; didn't liken my light
to kindness, my kindness to a light,
nor see much fair reply in those terms,
when I gave away more than I wanted;
didn't load up the furnace with names
I knew better than to circulate,
but kept my bitchy counsel via text
and enjoyed the absolute behaviour.
I don't know how the aperture works.
Just hope to blink one day and – green.
That the cool does its cool eventual thing.
And that my name. And that my loving.

But I know what I like

for Morgan Parker

The stakes are so low they couldn't be higher.
Which is why the brushwork matters.
Rehearsing facial expressions, chewing salad
all evening, pep and charm until everyone
has left, and the room is safe again . . .
If art makes us happy it's because
we let it win. We should reserve the right
to be petty. We know the true pleasure
is in theory, the scrutable chat-show
of meta-language, abstract nouns, nudging
them around like battleships or cashews
on the bar. We take the sublime anywhere
we can get it: sitting on our sunglasses,
a failed high-five with a child, not being
a dick to anyone today, or black coffee.
Let's put our made-up names on the tenancy
of history and see how long before anyone
notices, how long they let us stay, drunk
swans, very conspicuous. The shit-real truth
is, some friends live far away; you meet them
for a week and an evening, hope the gods
have it minuted because the future may not
be our penthouse. *Welp*. Let's be willing
to dream one: arriving with sunflowers,
dads at the grill, our people our people, or
just to cut the weed one day with rosemary,
all those big blue notes lifting into summer.

This time

it's going to be great! God called out to his wife. – *I know I've said it before, but I think I'm really onto something. I'm going to give them a linear sense of time, just one direction, all the way!* – *What?* Mrs God replied, arriving in the doorway where the garage meets the utility room, adjoining the kitchen – *but that's hardly anything at all?* she said, bemused, placing one of two plates with neatly cut sandwiches, each with a pile of assorted accompanying pickles, down on the workbench. – *I know! But that way they'll have beginnings and endings! Think how dramatic that will be! They'll need neat little bodies to inhabit, perhaps starting off small and new then growing larger, then more prone to malfunction, until they fail and each of them disappears down the chute, whoosh! I know it seems like a brutal constraint but it'll create pressure, dynamism, I mean, think how many of them will never meet, lovers kept a thousand years apart by a cruel lottery of ordering! And the great meandering conversations, stratified, strung out across the epochs, new voices, inflections, accents and terminologies joining all the time, just as the older voices and languages slide from memory, one gigantic melting block of ice that none will ever see even a corner of. Just imagine the intensity of that narrowed, sharpened experience. What a trip!* God grabbed the sandwich and chewed madly, scrutinising the sketches he had made. – *They'll be popping off like champagne bottles, they'll be out of their tiny minds!* Mrs God rolled her eyes, taking her identical sandwich and pickle assortment back indoors where the afternoon stretched like a cat between naps.

Big Shout Out

to the animals of the ocean
and the vast pressures surrounding
them reassuringly; to the sky looking
great in its harness, and relief,
my favourite emotion;
to the drop-in centre, all-night vigil
at the corner shop; to figure skaters
rehearsing afterhours, running
their routines in headphones
on a night-bus; to the requiem,
days and horizons on the slide,
and the cold, still circuit boards
in every dead satellite;
to remembering names correctly;
to the new coats of paint
on all the gates of heaven.

Lying on the floor of the supermarket

There is a factory where tape is fed
onto cardboard tubes all through the night,
a combine harvester puts its long arm out
into floodlights, productivity equals products:
the supermarket. I miss you, what more
can I say? That I have You-dreams
and Other-dreams.

In the Other-dreams I am mostly finding toilets
overflowing in high school or cradling
a faceless baby through the breakers.
In You-dreams I'm lying on the floor
of the supermarket. Like this.
With the same aubergines shining dully
in large green trays, the apples in bags of six,
wondering, *What would all that milk look like
emptied down a marble staircase?*

And that's when you reply over the tannoy,
*Like a marble staircase emptied down a marble
staircase. Wait. Another voice is coming, will be
softer than I.* But I don't want another voice.
I want your voice. Productivity is leaving me.
The plastic floor reciprocates the heat
of my back, the softer voice arriving now,
a red shadow across my eyelids, *Can I help you?
Can you move? Are you in need of help?
Can someone please get this person some help?*

A Greyhound Levitates across the Street

or maybe I imagined that for you.

Poem Beginning with a Line by Yu Xuanji

Adapted from the translation by Jennifer Carpenter

And the parrot's words have not yet ceased in its cage.
And your wet shoes are steaming on the radiator.
And no one has asked you how your day went.
And an urge arrives to have your head in a headlock.
Or to spit your teeth into a metal bowl just to look up,
grinning blood, and say, 'I'm a very tough architect.
Don't fuck with my angles. I am precise and I sell
tenderness every day.' But the scented candle is helping,
and that pound feels solid in your pocket. Temperature
not uncomfortable and in your mind an email writes
itself, thank goodness – now you won't have to do it.
Those enrolled among the mortals can wait their turn.
The parrot is a millionaire of circumstance unrealised.
Only persons made of light-comprising-thought-
lessness-in-water can enter this place. So you let them.

Behind the Face of Great White Shark

Glass of water in the dawn kitchen.
Since we brought you home from the hospital
I have prayed these hours to a stub.
Please water. Please glass. Great White Shark
always sniffing out the small far blood
and all my murders and funerals out
for revision, mind circling the short grass
like a bored dog. *Keep your shit together*
picturing a perfect pentagon drawn
freehand, or fucking ambidextrously,
anything to blot the rat-gnawed forehead,
worms correlating, dark target areas.
Two weeks since the last Great White attack
and cowardy custard, in with the green beans,
Are you struggling? I admit I have been sick
since we met, pursuing this love-wound
like a moon beyond the windscreen.
Morning leans across us like the shadow
of a closing door. It's not your fault.
Eat your banana. I can keep you safe inland.
I can love you like an expert: my adamant
hands, the voice I lower and lighten,
my arm hair so alert, as the shark turns
its face again, no aspect to discern, no
inclination or decision, just you reaching
both arms up, distracting from the scent,
the plume, the lesser work of living.

There Is a Supermassive Black Hole Four Million Times the Mass of the Sun at the Centre of Our Galaxy and You Are Pregnant with Our Daughter

We are not unique, and we are.
Every galaxy has its warden.
Another fact is that the human mind
is not an all-purpose device.
It is natural to be overwhelmed.
Sometimes the summer needs a snow day.

The story of the mind is that we woke up
in caves and arranged our thoughts to make
these intersections, and subsequent minor-
league fixtures; now we have intimate
waxing salons, overage, offshore, diffidence,
failed special handshakes in the lobbies
of the pyramids, songs always in the charts,
you look different *tra-la* have you done
something different to yourself today?

The garden is crying, and I truly feel the mind
is not an all-purpose device.
Sometimes the sky needs its tattered flag.
It is natural to experience things as difficult.
The story of difficulty goes that it
was experienced, then spread across
the land like a more efficient language,
like a wet kind of money in love.
It is natural to be overwhelmed.
Love can be both the train and the silence
that follows it down the track.

The garden will stop eventually.
Meanwhile traffic remembers and forgets itself
on the road beyond the window.
I am so scared, aren't you?
There is a supermassive black hole four million times
the mass of the sun at the centre of our galaxy
and she already responds to our voices.

Alpha Step

A change to my usual sleeping position,
earth holding me close
like I'm something it loves.
I feel a murmur through the hedgerow,
old gods thawing from the permafrost.
Only a matter of time
before an empire falls
into the hands of an idiot
and there are more ways of saying things
than things worth saying;
only a matter of love to steer the wind,
which batters us daily, this only life
that climbs beyond unfashionable
beginnings, leaving us leaving it,
breathless software, a bite taken out
of the grand old narrative,
while our ghosts refuel mid-air.
Deep time. Lovely time.
The human print will not survive.
I mean like, woo, there it was.

Breckland

Everyone out here driving the coast
of a cold front, noticing good places
to dispose of a body. In a hundred years
or less, this whole forest will be underwater,
a landscape rescinded, salt convecting
in between the pines. Bad-weird.
Maybe legend never had it. Maybe a whale
will swim the length of a ruined cathedral.
On the dashboard a satellite guides us
home from Christmas; the baby
twitches in her sleep. So count me in
for the rupture, for putting the animal
down. Love has always been a loss
of risklessness, like a new sky installed,
huge and ceramic, an orchestral silence
behind each door. I have a lot of apologies
to tender, a lot of perfectly adequate foliage
I've laid to waste for the coherence
of a pleasing foreground. I deserve
all the leaky batteries of the infosphere
as much as the next sorry song.
I could have done more but I didn't.
Darling light, the horns are sounding.
Here comes a chorus. Happy New Year.